UPDATED CERTIFIED LEAN SIX SIGMA YELLOW BELT EXAM QUESTION & ANSWERS

A comprehensive Study guide for the Certified Lean Six Sigma Yellow Belt Certification exam, with practice test, essays, examination insights, solutions and tips.

Bruce M. Chapman

ALL RIGHT RESERVED @ 2024

Bruce M. Chapman

"All rights reserved. This publication is protected by copyright and may not be reproduced, stored in a retrieval system, or transmitted in any form or by any means—be it photocopying, recording, electronic, mechanical, or otherwise—without the express written permission of the copyright owner. The sole exceptions are brief quotations in critical articles or reviews."

Preface

Welcome to the ultimate resource for passing the Certified Lean Six Sigma Yellow Belt Certification exam. This painstakingly created manual goes above and beyond the call of duty to inspire and mentor learners as they pursue greatness. With great pleasure, I introduce "UPDATED CERTIFIED LEAN SIX SIGMA YELLOW BELT EXAM QUESTION & ANSWERS," a thorough study guide that goes beyond conventional exam preparation.

In the context of Lean Six Sigma, excellence is a standard that necessitates diligence, wisdom, and a thorough comprehension of the ideas that propel organizational success. With careful attention to detail, this guide offers prospective Yellow Belts a wealth of essays, practice exams, exam insights, solutions, and priceless advice, all thoughtfully chosen to improve your comprehension and performance.

This study guide covers every aspect of the Certified Lean Six Sigma Yellow Belt exam and goes beyond simply being a collection of questions and answers. Every part, from basic ideas to sophisticated techniques, is meant to improve your understanding and sharpen your problem-solving abilities.

Through insightful essays, get a deeper knowledge of important Lean Six Sigma ideas. These essays explore practical applications, giving you the knowledge required to successfully negotiate the challenges of process optimization and improvement.

Try your knowledge on carefully designed practice exams that simulate the real thing. These exams are learning aids intended to reinforce concepts and pinpoint areas in need of development; they are more than merely assessments.

Discover the subtleties of the Yellow Belt test with insightful knowledge. Recognize the format, question types, and attitude required to tackle each segment with assurance on the exam.

Go beyond providing accurate responses and learn the logic behind them. This guide will equip you to take on whatever obstacle the exam throws at you with comprehensive solutions and professional advice to help you understand the underlying ideas.

Students want to become proficient practitioners of Lean Six Sigma approaches, not only pass the Certified Lean Six Sigma Yellow Belt exam.

Professionals looking for a resource that offers a thorough grasp of Lean Six Sigma principles for real-world application in the workplace, going beyond simple exam preparation.

Set off on your Lean Six Sigma journey with assurance, having gained the knowledge and understanding necessary to succeed. This manual serves as more than just a study aid; it is also a catalyst for your development and your path to becoming a Certified Lean Six Sigma Yellow Belt. Now let's start learning.

Forward

When it comes to achieving excellence in the field of Lean Six Sigma, it is common to require an above-average reference that will not only help you pass the exam but also develop a deep comprehension of the concepts that support process optimization. I am excited to share with you the "UPDATED CERTIFIED LEAN SIX SIGMA YELLOW BELT EXAM QUESTION & ANSWERS."

This guide offers a thorough exploration of the core principles of Lean Six Sigma techniques, not just a collection of exam-focused content. This resource, which has been meticulously crafted with attention to detail, is intended to provide aspiring Yellow Belts with an extensive toolkit for success.

You will find a comprehensive method to learning that covers every topic on the Certified Lean Six Sigma Yellow Belt exam as you progress through the chapters. The incorporation of comprehensive essays facilitates a more profound comprehension of fundamental concepts, encouraging analytical reasoning and practical implementation.

The thoughtful placement of practice exams throughout the manual functions as both a wonderful learning resource and an assessment tool. Designed to replicate the real exam setting, these assessments highlight areas for growth and reinforce topics, guaranteeing a comprehensive study experience.

As you explore the test insights provided, you will develop a more sophisticated comprehension of the Yellow Belt exam. This section offers insightful viewpoints on test formats, question kinds, and the frame of mind required to confidently tackle each segment.

This guide includes solutions and advice throughout, providing more than just right answers. Every solution serves as a springboard for a greater understanding of Lean Six Sigma principles, equipping you to use your skillset productively in the workplace.

This handbook is designed for professionals who want to learn Lean Six Sigma approaches for real-world application in the workplace, as well as students who want to excel in the Certified Lean Six Sigma Yellow Belt exam. It acts as a road map, assisting you in understanding the nuances of Lean Six Sigma and establishing the foundation for ongoing development.

Set off on this adventure with assurance, equipped not just with the resources needed to pass a test but also with the knowledge and awareness necessary to succeed as a Certified Lean Six Sigma Yellow Belt. As you go toward a future of ongoing learning and operational excellence, let this guide be your constant companion. I hope your journey with Lean Six Sigma is rewarding and transformative.

Introduction

Choose from a variety of practice exams that have been meticulously created to closely resemble the format and content of the actual exam. By completing these tests, you can become accustomed to the structure and range of exam question types. To enhance comprehension and critical thinking, look for essay themes that are thorough and contain a lot of CLSSYB components.

The book also includes the hand-picked professionals with outstanding exam results who have provided insightful advice and assistance. Pay special attention to the following tips to make sure you understand the subjects covered in the test and the most effective ways to solve issues.

Our intention is for you to pass the CLSSYB Exam by using this book as a helpful resource. Hopefully, you'll finish the task and pass the test. Start the primary course of action by taking the necessary activity. Once this step is completed, success is assured. Let's get going now!

TIPS FOR THE CLSSYB EXAM:

1. Become familiar with the core concepts, tenets, and terminology of the CLSSYB Framework.

2. You'll be better prepared for exams by taking practice exams. This is a great method to familiarize yourself with the format and types of questions that will appear on the test. These exercises could also point up areas where someone needs to strengthen their competencies.

3. Acquire a thorough understanding of every topic addressed on the CLSSYB Exam to focus your study efforts on the topics that are most likely to be asked about.

4. Keep in mind that the CLSSYB Exam has a time constraint. Make sure you complete each question within the allocated time by employing effective time management strategies.

5. Although exam anxiety is common, maintaining composure and concentration will improve your performance significantly on the CLSSYB Exam.

BENEFITS OF CLSSYB EXAM

1. Improved Ability to Solve Problems: Through the use of a methodical and data-driven approach to process improvement, the Certified Lean Six Sigma Yellow Belt exam hones participants' problem-solving skills. This skill set is very helpful in recognizing and resolving organizational operational issues.

2. Operational Efficiency Improvement: Those who pass the test will have the information necessary to maximize efficiency, cut waste, and streamline procedures. This immediately boosts overall productivity, lowers expenses, and improves operational performance.

3. Opportunities for job Advancement: Having a Certified Lean Six Sigma Yellow Belt certification gives you access to a lot of different job paths. Professionals who can contribute to efforts for continuous improvement are valued by employers, which helps certified individuals stand out on the job market and offers opportunities for career advancement.

4. Standardized Methodology: By guaranteeing that everyone have a consistent language and toolkit, the exam transmits a standardized methodology for process improvement. This standardization encourages teamwork and communication, which leads to a cohesive and successful problem-solving strategy.

5. Organizational Competitiveness: Businesses that use Lean Six Sigma techniques frequently have a market advantage. In the fast-paced corporate world of today, those who hold a Certified Lean Six Sigma Yellow Belt certification are essential to an organization's dedication to quality, customer happiness, and general competitiveness.

1. What ratio is commonly followed by the data displayed by the Pareto Chart?

      A. 70:30

      B. 80:20

      C. 90:10

      D. 95:5

Answer : **B**

2. From his neighborhood electronics store, Al purchased a handheld GPS. He tried entering an address, but it didn't work. What kind of expense would this fall under for the GPS manufacturer?

    A. Internal Failure Cost

    B. Prevention Cost

    C. External Failure Cost

    D. Appraisal Cost

Answer : **C**

3. Which of the following best describes how the idea that a process's outputs are a function of all of its inputs is expressed?

    A. $Y = f(Xn)$

    B. RTY > 90%

    C. Yield = Effort

    D. Flow = Demand

Answer : **A**

4. The _____ symbol is used to represent an action step in the process while creating a process map.

      A. Diamond

      B. Circle

      C. Ellipse

      D. Rectangle

Answer : **D**

5. A Belt has concluded that the loan application does not require an accounting review, which increases the volume of applications a loan processor may process.

RTY improvement is defined in terms of Cost of Poor Quality (COPQ) as _____.

    A. Downsizing savings

    B. Hard savings

    C. Soft savings

    D. Median savings

Answer : **B**

6. The business case that follows is appropriately put together.

In contrast to its goal of almost no returns, Division 16 saw 4.2% of products returned over the most of 2008. The business has a heavy financial burden as a result.

A. True

B. False

Answer : **B**

7. Focusing efforts on _____ and streamlining processes to attain speed and agility at a reduced cost is the core of lean methodology.

       A. Defect removal

       B. Removing waste

       C. Overtime reduction

       D. Rework reduction

Answer : **B**

8. A Belt added a feature to the process map named _____ after realizing that the procedure involved several departments.

   A. Passing Lanes
   B. Swim Lanes
   C. Department Dividers
   D. Responsibility Paths

Answer : **B**

9. One of the main goals we have when designing and defining an LSS project is to decrease the _____.

    A. Work force

    B. Number of process steps

    C. Inventory

    D. Cost of Poor Quality

Answer : **D**

10. An organization's value chain is the culmination of all the procedures that are used to transform inputs into the required outputs that customers need.

    A. True

    B. False

Answer : **A**

11. The DPMO, or _____, is a crucial Six Sigma statistic.

    A. Delayed production metrics output

    B. Defects by management oversight

    C. Defects per million opportunities

    D. Developed production management oversight

Answer : **C**

12. Which of the following is a typical term for business KPIs, such as cycle time, defects, scrap cost, and safety?

      A. Defects per Unit

      B. Key Performance Indicators

      C. Impediments to Flow

      D. Hidden Costs

Answer : **B**

13. In order to create a Fishbone Diagram that encompasses all relevant topics, it is recommended that your team employ the _____ method.

    A. Graphical

    B. Data collection

    C. Shewhart

    D. Brainstorming

Answer : **D**

14. Which of the following tools is produced using a 5 Why Analysis to help uncover potential fault causes?

    A. Fishbone Diagram

    B. SIPOC

    C. X-Y Matrix

    D. Pareto Chart

Answer : **A**

15. A process map's objectives are to determine the process's complexity and to help locate _____ inside the process.

A. Critical steps

B. Line operators

C. Test stations

D. Defects

Answer : **A**

16. We are instructed to walk a project through from start to finish in the outset. To _____, we take this action.

    A. Meet the workers

    B. Draft a Process Map

    C. See what inventory is involved

    D. Check the repair stations

Answer : **B**

17. The primary purpose of the Method category on a Fishbone Diagram related to Root Causes is to produce concepts regarding potential sources of flaws by the _____.

    A. Inventory management

    B. Effects of the environment

    C. Way work is done

    D. Parts or forms used

Answer : **C**

18. A _____ is used in Process Map creation to indicate the direction of work flow.

    A. Solid line arrow

    B. Dashed line arrow

    C. Series of dots

    D. Double lines

Answer : **A**

19. Remember that there are essentially three perspectives on a process at the start of a project: what you THINK it is, what it ACTUALLY is, and what is documented.

    A. True

    B. False

Answer : **B**

20. One of the main results of a SIPOC is to start figuring out which inputs have the biggest impact on the _____ most valuable outputs.

    A. Business's

    B. Employee's

    C. Management's

    D. Customer's

Answer : **D**

21. A department's whole set of operations may be mapped out in a Macro Process Map, which may also be divided into several Micro Process Maps that represent the various processes that make up the department's activities.

    A. True

    B. False

Answer : **A**

22. Suppliers, Inputs, _____, Output, and Customers make up the acronym SIPOC.

    A. Production

    B. Process

    C. Products

    D. Presentation

Answer : **B**

23. We start to identify some steps that are NVA, or non-violent audits, as we start to use a process map to explain what's happening with our process.

      A. Non-value add

      B. No violation allowed

      C. Non-value actions

      D. Next vehicle action

Answer : **A**

24. We are encouraged to apply the RUMBA approach—which stands for Reasonable, Understandable, _____, Believable, and Achievable—when determining the needs from customers and suppliers for a SIPOC.

A. Manageable

B. Massive

C. Memorable

D. Measurable

Answer : **D**

25. The term "_____" refers to inputs that are random in nature, impossible to measure, and may have a minor impact on your process.

    A. Nuisance

    B. Noise

    C. Pests

    D. Elusive

Answer : **B**

26. The entire range of variation that can be anticipated from the subject process's output is represented by the long-term data.

    A. True

    B. False

Answer : **A**

27. A line operator is measuring the temperature of a liquid. Which is the least susceptible to the instrument's influence?

       A. Recording the measurement

       B. Actual temperature of the liquid

       C. Calibration of the instrument

       D. Reading of the instrument

Answer : **A**

28. The fact that the data gathered from this exercise is precise and certain is one of the main advantages of your team working together to produce an X-Y diagram.

    A. True

    B. False

Answer : **B**

29. Measurement system analysis is a process that measures variations in the system or method used to gather measurements and ensures that useful data is obtained.

   A. True

   B. False

Answer : **A**

30. In order to create a Pareto chart, a Belt collected the following defect data for a production line that made pants. The following would be the proper sequence on the chart, left to right:

Data:Cutting29 -

Forming43 -

Stitching17 -

Sealing51 -

    A. Sealing, Forming, Cutting, Stitching

    B. Cutting, Stitching, Sealing, Forming

    C. Stitching, Forming, Cutting, Sealing

    D. Forming, Cutting, Sealing, Stitching

Answer : **A**

31. Sorting the important few Xs from the unimportant many Xs is one of the main goals of creating an X-Y diagram.

    A. True

    B. False

Answer : **A**

32. A set of data is referred to as _____ if it is broadly distributed yet largely centered in relation to the desired value.

       A. Precise but not accurate

       B. Accurate but not precise

       C. Precise but skewed

       D. Accurate but distributed

Answer : **B**

33. The characteristics of a measurement system are defined by its accuracy, linearity, and bias.

    A. Sensitivity

    B. Repeatability

    C. Accuracy

    D. Precision

    Answer : **C**

34. The _____ is a tool we use to find potential failures (defects) in our process and the potential effects they may have.

    A. Shewhart Analysis

    B. Juran Journey

    C. FMEA

    D. SIPOC

Answer : **C**

35. The different Failure Modes are ranked according to how they affect the process's output using the RPN, or Risk Priority Number.

    A. True

    B. False

Answer : **A**

36. The goal of _____ is to evaluate data and present it so that we may decide what is going on in our process with knowledge.

      A. Data Sampling

      B. Basic Statistics

      C. Calculating Standard Deviation

      D. Measurement System Analysis

Answer : **B**

37. Process capability is determined by the needs of the client, continuous output, and error-free performance.

    A. True

    B. False

Answer : **A**

38. The _____ particular areas in our processes where waste usually occurs are defined for us by Lean Principles.

    A. Three

    B. Five

    C. Seven

    D. Nine

Answer : **C**

39. It is advised that a 5S program be implemented throughout the facility after first being implemented in a pilot work area for educational and demonstration objectives.

    A. True

    B. False

Answer : **A**

40. To highlight areas that require organizing and cleaning, _____ are produced as part of a Visual Factory strategy.

    A. Flashing lights

    B. Soft horns

    C. Kanban cards

    D. Operator announcement programs

Answer : **C**

41. Reducing the amount of job tasks that are out of the ordinary and necessitate uncommon judgments and actions to complete the right things is one of the 5S ways to waste elimination. The name of this 5S gadget is _____.

    A. Standardizing

    B. Scheduling

    C. Sustaining

    D. Sorting

Answer : **A**

42. Keeping the _____ current is a good idea to support the Response Plan, as the Control Plan serves as a roadmap for maintaining the gains obtained during the Lean Six Sigma project.

A. X-Y Diagram

B. Shewhart Chart

C. FMEA

D. Customer Service Plan

Answer : **C**

43. Which of the following actions help us apply Lean Principles to reduce waste?

A. Organize tools and raw materials

B. Keep the work area clean and organized

C. Maintain a proper volume of inventory at hand

D. All of these answers are correct

Answer : **D**

44. The Lean Principle known as _____ asserts that reducing waste is an ongoing endeavor that necessitates constant awareness of methods to minimize the seven components of waste.

    A. Kaizen

    B. Ishikawa

    C. Kanban

    D. Muda

Answer : **A**

45. Determining who, when, and to what extent different persons must be engaged in order to maintain process improvements is a crucial component of a workable control plan.

   A. Transferred

   B. Promoted

   C. Trained

   D. Dismissed

Answer : **C**

46. After a project is over, a Belt has to finish the _____ and give the Process Owner accountability for it.

    A. Final Process Map

    B. Project Timesheet

    C. Team Briefing Paper

    D. Documentation Plan

Answer : **D**

47. Which of the following best describes the processes and systems that enable people to permanently alter their behavior?

      A. Documented performance objectives

      B. Defined procedures

      C. Accurate job descriptions

      D. Incentive compensation

      E. All of these answers are correct

Answer : **E**

48. When the Measure Phase is complete, the Control Plan is made. When may it be closed?

    A. After the project costs have been recouped

    B. When the Champion says so

    C. Never, a Control Plan must stay in place

    D. At the fiscal yearend of the business

Answer : **C**

49. The best way to decrease operator or person-introduced flaws into a process is for a Belt to devise and apply a way to _____ into the process.

    A. Measurement automation

    B. Operator alertness

    C. Full Automation

    D. Constant supervision

Answer : **C**

50. At the end of a project, a monitoring plan will be implemented to ensure that there are sufficient systems with critical metric readouts showing conditions that are outside of specification.

    A. True

    B. False

Answer : **A**

51. What is Lean Six Sigma, and how does it combine Six Sigma and Lean methodology principles?

_____

_____

_____

_____

_____

_____

_____

_____

_____

_____

_____

52. Give a definition of DMAIC and discuss each step in terms of process enhancement.

53. What are the common tools for measuring and controlling variation, and how does the notion fit into Six Sigma?

54. Describe the distinction between a process's special cause variation and common cause variation.

_____

_____

_____

_____

_____

_____

_____

_____

_____

_____

55. Explain the rationale for and advantages of developing a process map during the DMAIC Define phase.

56. In a Lean Six Sigma project, what are a Yellow Belt's primary duties?

_____

_____

_____

_____

_____

_____

_____

_____

_____

_____

57. How does the DMAIC framework's use of root cause analysis aid in problem-solving?

58. Talk about the value of stakeholder analysis in a project that uses Lean Six Sigma methodology.

59. How does the use of Six Sigma principles involve statistical thinking?

60. Describe the function of control charts and how they are used in process monitoring and control.

61. Explain what CTQ (Critical to Quality) is and give instances of CTQ criteria in various sectors.

62. Talk about how crucial it is to analyze measuring devices and gather data during the Measure phase.

_____

_____

_____

_____

_____

_____

_____

_____

_____

_____

_____

63. What do process capability indices tell you about a process, and how are they calculated?

64. Explain the 5S tenets and how Lean workplace organization relates to them.

_____

_____

_____

_____

_____

_____

_____

_____

_____

_____

65. Describe the Poka-Yoke concept and give instances of how it has been applied in a process.

_____

_____

_____

_____

_____

_____

_____

_____

_____

_____

66. What is a fishbone diagram, and how is it applied in Lean Six Sigma to identify problems?

67. Talk about how the Pareto chart helps prioritize problems during process optimization.

_____

_____

_____

_____

_____

_____

_____

_____

_____

_____

_____

68. Explain what kaizen is and why it matters for attempts to improve continuously.

69. What role does Failure Mode and Effects Analysis, or FMEA, play in a process' risk assessment?

70. Describe the differences and applications of SIPOC diagrams and process maps.

71. In Lean Six Sigma projects, what role does the Voice of the Customer (VOC) play?

_____

_____

_____

_____

_____

_____

_____

_____

_____

_____

72. How does the DMAIC's Analyze phase decision-making process benefit from hypothesis testing?

73. Explain what Takt time is and how it relates to scheduling and production planning.

74. Describe the idea of standard work and how it affects process enhancement and stability.

_____

_____

_____

_____

_____

_____

_____

_____

_____

_____

75. Talk about the fundamentals of error-proofing and how to use it to cut down on errors.

_____

_____

_____

_____

_____

_____

_____

_____

_____

_____

76. How can the application of control plans help maintain the gains made in a Lean Six Sigma project?

_____

_____

_____

_____

_____

_____

_____

_____

_____

_____

77. Explain lead and lag indicators in process performance measurement and give instances.

78. Describe the role that Gage R&R (Repeatability and Reproducibility) plays in the examination of measuring systems.

79. Talk on the value of cooperation and team dynamics in Lean Six Sigma initiatives.

80. How is the application of regression analysis related to process improvement?

81. Explain what a "Black Belt" is in the context of Lean Six Sigma and what a project manager does.

_____

_____

_____

_____

_____

_____

_____

_____

_____

_____

82. Talk about the Lean thinking concepts of Muda, Mura, and Muri and how they affect productivity.

_____

_____

_____

_____

_____

_____

_____

_____

_____

_____

83. Describe the distinctions between quantitative and qualitative data and how Six Sigma projects might benefit from them.

84. How important is benchmarking to the process of continuous improvement?

85. Talk about the fundamentals of value stream mapping and how it helps find waste in processes.

_____

_____

_____

_____

_____

_____

_____

_____

_____

_____

86. Describe the relationship between Lean and the notion of Total Productive Maintenance (TPM).

87. What connection exists between process variability and control and the idea of standard deviation?

88. Outline the procedures for developing and maintaining a process control strategy.

_____

_____

_____

_____

_____

_____

_____

_____

_____

_____

_____

89. How is a process capacity study carried out, and what is its aim?

90. Talk about how crucial communication is to a Lean Six Sigma project's success.

_____

_____

_____

_____

_____

_____

_____

_____

_____

_____

91. Describe the distinction between a process's systemic and random fluctuation.

92. In what ways might error-proofing methods help a manufacturing process reduce errors?

_____

_____

_____

_____

_____

_____

_____

_____

_____

_____

93. Explain what a "critical path" is and why it matters in project management.

_____

_____

_____

_____

_____

_____

_____

_____

_____

_____

94. Talk about the Just-In-Time (JIT) production philosophies and how they affect inventory control.

95. How does brainstorming fit into the Define phase of the DMAIC, and how can it be done well?

_____

_____

_____

_____

_____

_____

_____

_____

_____

_____

96. Describe the idea of a batch and queue and how lean production principles apply to it.

97. Talk about how risk-mitigation techniques fit into the DMAIC Improve phase.

98. How is statistical process control related to the concept of standard deviation?

___

99. Explain what "cycle time" is and why it matters for process optimization.

_____

_____

_____

_____

_____

_____

_____

_____

_____

_____

100. Describe maturity models and how they are used in the context of Lean Six Sigma.

_____

_____

_____

_____

_____

_____

_____

_____

_____

_____

_____

Printed in Poland
by Amazon Fulfillment
Poland Sp. z o.o., Wrocław